LET'S PLAY
Football

Karen Durrie

MEDIA ENHANCED BOOKS
AV2 BY WEIGL
ADDED VALUE · AUDIO VISUAL

www.av2books.com

Go to **www.av2books.com**, and enter this book's unique code.

BOOK CODE

G 5 3 2 5 0 6

AV² by **Weigl** brings you media enhanced books that support active learning.

AV² provides enriched content that supplements and complements this book. Weigl's AV² books strive to create inspired learning and engage young minds in a total learning experience.

Your AV² Media Enhanced books come alive with...

Audio
Listen to sections of the book read aloud.

Video
Watch informative video clips.

Embedded Weblinks
Gain additional information for research.

Try This!
Complete activities and hands-on experiments.

Key Words
Study vocabulary, and complete a matching word activity.

Quizzes
Test your knowledge.

Slide Show
View images and captions, and prepare a presentation.

...and much, much more!

Published by AV² by Weigl
350 5th Avenue, 59th Floor New York, NY 10118
Website: www.av2books.com   www.weigl.com

Durrie, Karen.
 Football / Karen Durrie.
   p. cm. -- (Let's play)
 ISBN 978-1-61690-939-0 (hardcover : alk. paper) -- ISBN 978-1-61913-026-5 (pbk) -- ISBN 978-1-61690-585-9 (online)
 1. Football--Juvenile literature. I. Title.
 GV950.7.D87 2011
 796.332--dc23
                           2011023430

Printed in the United States of America in North Mankato, Minnesota
2 3 4 5 6 7 8 9 0 17 16 15 14 13

032013
WEP040313

Project Coordinator: Karen Durrie   Art Director: Terry Paulhus

Weigl acknowledges Getty Images as the primary image supplier for this title.

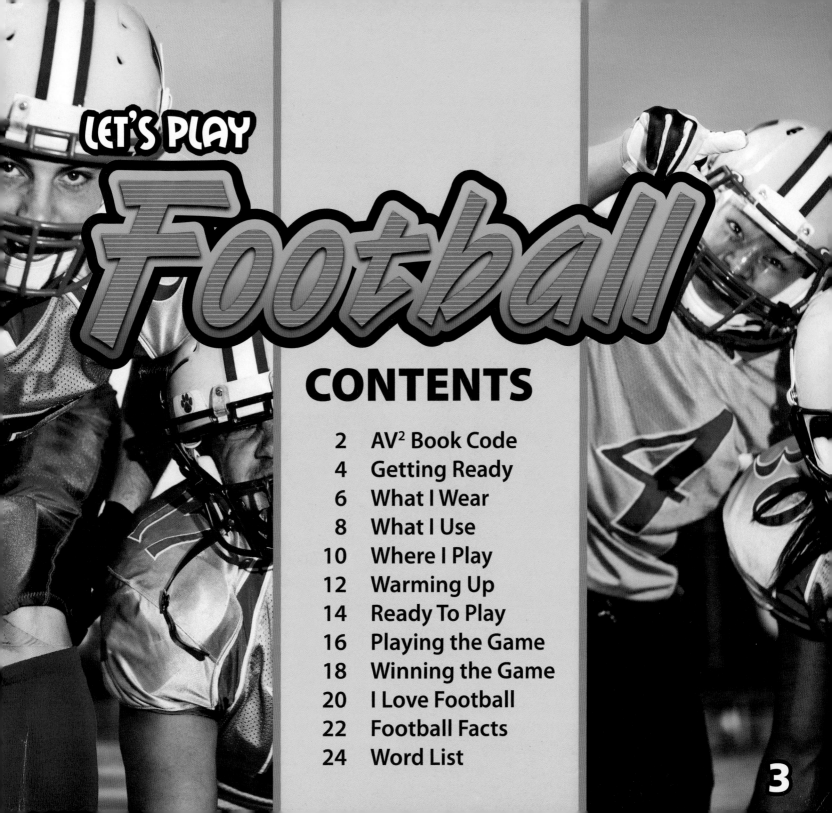

LET'S PLAY Football

CONTENTS

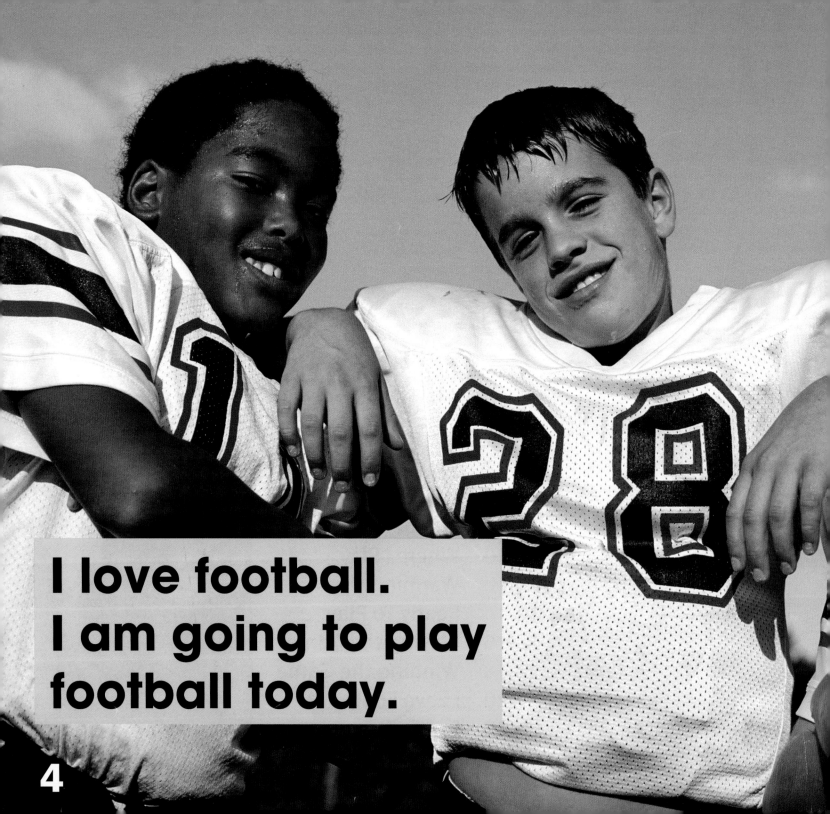

I love football.
I am going to play
football today.

4

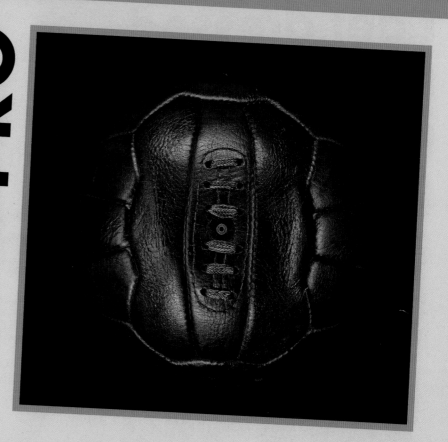

Football was first played with a soccer ball.

5

I get dressed
for football.
I put on pads.
I put on my green jersey.

6

Like a PRO

I wear pads and a helmet so I do not get hurt.

I have a football.
It is brown and shaped
like an egg.
It has laces.

Laces help me grip the ball. I need a good grip to throw the football.

I go to the field.
I meet my friends.
We are a team.

Like a PRO

Football fields are as long as a blue whale.

I run with my team.
I play catch with my team
before the game.

I warm up my muscles before I play.

13

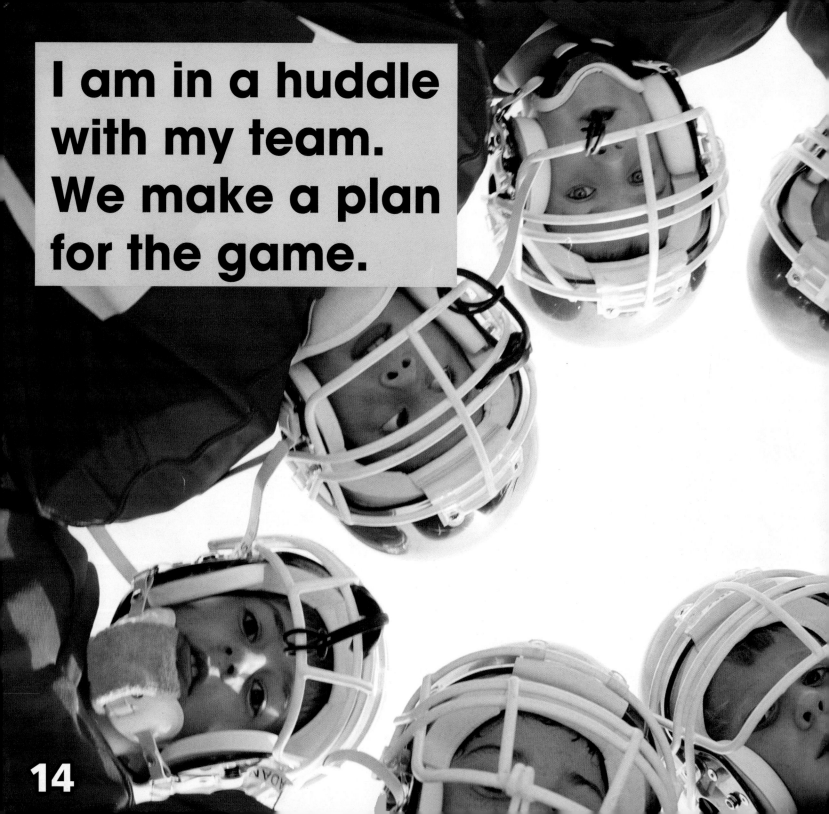

I am in a huddle with my team. We make a plan for the game.

Like a PRO

Players have different jobs to do on the field.

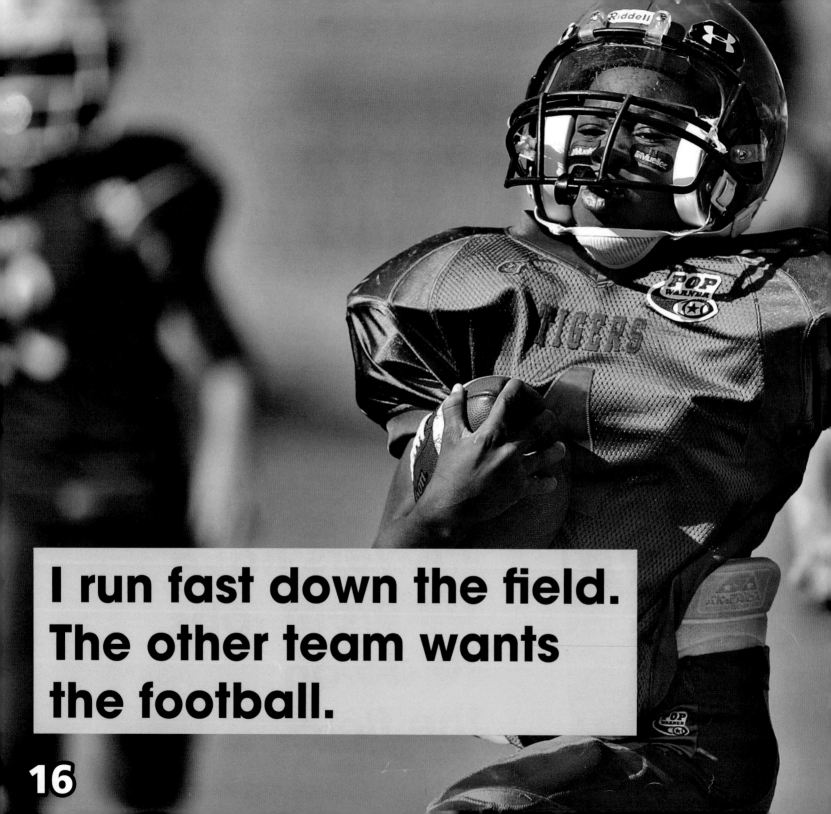

I run fast down the field.
The other team wants
the football.

The other team tackles us and blocks the ball.

I take the ball to the end of the field.
I score a touchdown.

Some players jump for joy after making a touchdown.

I love football.

FOOTBALL FACTS

This page provides more detail about the interesting facts found in the book.
Simply look at the corresponding page number to match the fact.

Pages 4-5

Football is more than 100 years old. It originated in England from sport called rugby. Rugby was played at American colleges in the mid-1800s, where players made some important changes. They used an egg-shaped ball and kept score differently. They renamed the new sport football.

Pages 6–7

Football is a contact sport. It can get rough, so protective equipment is important. Players wear pads to protect their ribs, arms, shoulders, and legs. They wear helmets with a wire cage at the front and a mouthguard. They also wear football cleats.

Pages 8–9

Throwing a football takes a lot of practice. Players are taught a proper football grip, and learn how throw good passes, including a spiral, where the ball spins as it flies.

Pages 10–11

Football fields have white lines to mark the boundaries and the distance traveled by players. A team must move the ball down the field in order to get more chances to score a touchdown.

Pages 12–13

Cold muscles are stiff, and sudden twisting and turning of them can cause injury. Warming and stretching muscles before playing football can reduce the risk of injury. Warm muscles also produce more energy faster. This helps a player run faster and perform with more accuracy and skill.

Pages 14–15

A huddle is a tight circle the team forms on the field before a play starts. The quarterback's job is to call plays during the huddle and to make sure all of his or her teammates understand the play.

Pages 16–17

Tackle football leagues start at age 5. Players are taught never to lead with their heads when tackling and are shown proper form for blocking and tackling. There is football that does not allow tackling. In flag football, players wear belts with flags attached by velcro. Pulling the flag off a player is the same as tackling in contact football.

Pages 18–19

The main goal in football is to score touchdowns. A touchdown is scored when a player runs across the end zone with the ball. Another way to score points is to kick field goals through the goal posts.

Pages 20–21

If a football game is won, it is the team that wins, not just the players that had touchdowns or kicked field goals. Cheering your team, as well as giving the other team a cheer or handshake at the end of a game, is part of good sportsmanship.

WORD LIST

Research has shown that as much as 65 percent of all written material published in English is made up of 300 words. These 300 words cannot be taught using pictures or learned by sounding them out. They must be recognized by sight. This book contains 44 common sight words to help young readers improve their reading fluency and comprehension. This book also teaches young readers several important content words. These words are paired with pictures to aid in learning and improve understanding.

Page	Sight Words First Appearance	Page	Content Words First Appearance
4	I, play, to	4	football, today
5	a, first, was, with	5	ball, soccer
6	for, get, on, put, my	6	jersey, pads
7	and, so, do, get, not	7	helmet
8	an, have, it, like	8	egg, laces
9	good, help, need, the	10	field, friends, team
10	are, friends, go, we	11	fields, whale
11	as, long	12	game
12	before, run	13	muscles
13	up	14	huddle, plan
14	in, make	15	jobs, players
16	down, other, wants	18	end, touchdown
18	end, of, take	19	joy
19	after, some		

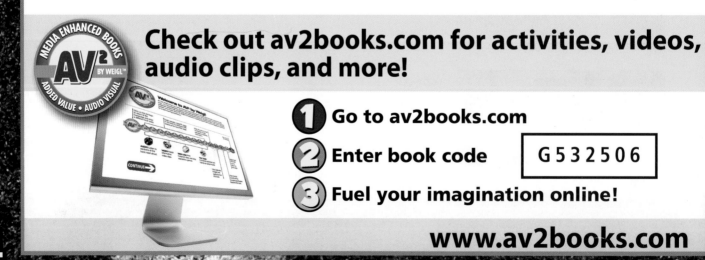

www.av2books.com